The Sign In The Subway

CARVETH MITCHELL

C.S.S. Publishing Co., Inc.
Lima, Ohio

THE SIGN IN THE SUBWAY

Copyright © 1988 by
The C.S.S. Publishing Company, Inc.
Lima, Ohio

All rights reserved. No part of this publication may be reproduced, stored in a retrieval system, or transmitted in any form or by any means, electronic, mechanical, photocopying, recording, or otherwise, without the prior permission of the publisher. Inquiries should be addressed to: The C.S.S. Publishing Company, Inc., 628 South Main Street, Lima, Ohio 45804.

Library of Congress Cataloging-in-Publication Data

Mitchell, Carveth P.
   The sign in the subway.

   1. Church year sermons.   2. Evangelical Lutheran Church in America — Sermons.   3. Lutheran Church — Sermons.   4. Sermons, American.   I. Title.
BX8333.M54S54   1988   252'.6   88-2867
ISBN 1-55673-056-X

8853 / ISBN 1-55673-056-X

Table of Contents

Lectionary Preaching After Pentecost		7
Proper 10[1] Pentecost 8[2] Ordinary Time 15[3]	*The Nearest Hand* *Luke 10:25-37*	10
Proper 11 Pentecost 9 Ordinary Time 16	*Complaint from the Kitchen* *Luke 10:38-42*	16
Proper 12 Pentecost 10 Ordinary Time 17	*The Sign in the Subway* *Luke 11:1-13*	21
Proper 13 Pentecost 11 Ordinary Time 18	*The Foolish Farmer* *Luke 12:13-21*	27
Proper 14 Pentecost 12 Ordinary Time 19	*The Emperor's Son-in-law* *Luke 12:32-40*[1,2] *Luke 12:32-48*[3]	32
Proper 15 Pentecost 13 Ordinary Time 20	*Our Splintered World* *Luke 12:49-56*[1] *Luke 12:49-53*[2,3]	37
Proper 16 Pentecost 14 Ordinary Time 21	*The Turnstile at the Pearly Gate* *Luke 13:22-30*	42
Proper 17 Pentecost 15 Ordinary Time 22	*The Man Who Came to Dinner* *Luke 14:1, 7-14*	47
Proper 18 Pentecost 16 Ordinary Time 23	*I Voted for God* *Luke 14:25-33*	52
Proper 19 Pentecost 17 Ordinary Time 24	*Dodging the Thrust* *Luke 15:1-10*	57

Proper 20 **Pentecost 18** **Ordinary Time 25**	*Jesus and the Rascal* *Luke 16:1-13*	62
Proper 21 **Pentecost 19** **Ordinary Time 26**	*The Man Who Didn't Care* *Luke 16:19-31*	67
Proper 22 **Pentecost 20** **Ordinary Time 27**	*No Snap Courses* *Luke 17:5-10*[1,3] *Luke 17:1-10*[2]	72

[1] Common Lectionary
[2] Lutheran Lectionary
[3] Roman Catholic Lectionary

Lectionary Preaching After Pentecost

Virtually all pastors who make use of the sermons in this book will find their worship life and planning shaped by one of two lectionary series. Most mainline Protestant denominations, along with clergy of the Roman Catholic Church, have now approved — either for provisional or official use — the three-year Common (Consensus) Lectionary. This family of denominations includes United Methodist, Presbyterian, United Church of Christ, and Disciples of Christ.

Lutherans and Roman Catholics, while testing the Common Lectionary on a limited basis at present, follow their own three-year cycle of texts. While there are divergences between the Common and Lutheran/Roman Catholic systems, the gospel texts show striking parallels, with few text selections evidencing significant differences. Virtually all the gospel texts included in this book will, therefore, be applicable to worship and preaching planning for clergy following either lectionary.

A significant divergence does occur, however, in the method by which specific gospel texts are assigned to specific calendar days. The Common and Roman Catholic lectionaries accomplish this by counting backwards from Christ the King (Last Sunday after Pentecost), discarding "extra" texts from the front of the list; Lutherans follow the opposite pattern, counting forward from The Holy Trinity, discarding "extra" texts at the end of the list.

The following index will aid the user of this book in matching the right text to the right Sunday during the "Pentecost Half" of the church year (days listed here include only those appropriate to this book's contents):

Fixed Date Lectionaries   **Lutheran Lectionary**

Text Designation

Common   *Roman Catholic*

Proper 10   Ordinary Time 15   Pentecost 8
    July 10-16
Proper 11   Ordinary Time 16   Pentecost 9
    July 17-23

Proper 12 *July 24-30*	Ordinary Time 17	Pentecost 10
Proper 13 *July 31 — August 6*	Ordinary Time 18	Pentecost 11
Proper 14 *August 7-13*	Ordinary Time 19	Pentecost 12
Proper 15 *August 14-20*	Ordinary Time 20	Pentecost 13
Proper 16 *August 21-27*	Ordinary Time 21	Pentecost 14
Proper 17 *August 28 — September 3*	Ordinary Time 22	Pentecost 15
Proper 18 *September 4-10*	Ordinary Time 23	Pentecost 16
Proper 19 *September 11-17*	Ordinary Time 24	Pentecost 17
Proper 20 *September 18-24*	Ordinary Time 25	Pentecost 18
Proper 21 *September 25 — October 1*	Ordinary Time 26	Pentecost 19
Proper 22 *October 2-8*	Ordinary Time 27	Pentecost 20

To Kathryn

*wife, companion, helpmate and inspiration
through fifty years of ministry*

Luke 10:25-37

Proper 10 (C)
Pentecost 8 (L)
Ordinary Time 15 (RC)

The Nearest Hand

Two women were sitting in church. One woman said to the other, "I've always wished that God would touch me, but I suppose that's too much to ask."

The other woman replied, "That sounds like a reasonable desire. Have you prayed about it?"

"Well, no. Of course not."

"Why not? There's certainly nothing wrong with a prayer like that. You should pray about it."

"All right. Maybe I will sometime."

"Not sometime. Now. What better place to pray than here in the Lord's house?"

Thus persuaded, the woman reluctantly folded her hands, bowed her head and closed her eyes in prayer, asking that God would touch her. About ten seconds later the other woman gently laid her hand on the folded hands of the friend at prayer. She responded as most of us would do. She jumped and said, "He did it! He touched me." Then, after a moment's thought "But that felt an awful lot like *your* hand."

"It *was* my hand," her friend replied.

Disappointment was on the other face. "And I thought God had touched me."

"He *did* touch you. How do you think God touches people? That he comes down like a fog blanket or a pillar of fire? When God touches people he takes the nearest hand and uses that."

That sounds good, doesn't it? And it's almost right. Almost, but not quite. She left out one word. When God touches people he takes the nearest *willing* hand and uses that. The Gospel for today is a case in point. The nearest hand to the stricken traveler was the hand of the priest, but it wasn't a *willing* hand. The next nearest hand was the hand of the Levite, but it was not a willing hand, either. The nearest *willing* hand was the hand of the Samaritan, so God took that hand and touched the stricken traveler in the ditch.

Jesus said of himself, "The Son of man came not to *be* served, but to serve." (Matthew 10:28) He said of us who follow him, "Whoever would be great among you must be your servant." (Mark 10:43, 45)

When God touches people he takes the nearest willing hand and uses that. This is one of the basic outgrowths of the Christian faith. When we forget that basic principle some dire consequences result. One such consequence is that we fail to see the hand of God at all.

In our city a husband and wife and two children lived in a small frame bungalow. Their heat was supplied by a pot-bellied stove. In the severe winter weather the house caught fire, destroying most of the structure, as well as furniture and clothing. The family was not injured. The newspaper told about their plight. Neighbors and church people from all over the city responded. Soon they had a place to live, useable furniture and sufficient food.

When I visited the family to see if anything more was needed, the wife said, "The Lord really has been good to us in our trouble."

The husband chuckled a bit and said, "I ain't seen the Lord doin' much, but the neighbors really kicked in."

You see? Because he had not realized that when the Lord touches people he takes the nearest willing hand and uses that, he failed to see the hand of God at all.

There is a second consequence of our failure to remember this basic principle: when the nearest hand is our own, if it is not a willing hand we deny our Lord and blunt the work that he would do through us.

It is our Christian faith that God reveals himself to us in three ways: as Creator, Redeemer and Sanctifier. To sanctify means to "make holy" — to lead us to become instruments of God, through whom he does his work, to be his willing hands.

Antonio Stradivari lived a long time ago. (1644-1737) Even now people both inside and outside the music world are familiar with the name and the fame (and the enormous cost!) of Stradivari's violins. He is reported to have said,

> *When any master holds twixt chin and hand a violin of mine, he will be glad that Stradivari lived — lived and made violins, and made them of the best — God choosing me to help him. If my hand slacked, I should rob God, since God could not make Antonio's violins without Antonio.*

When our hand is the nearest to some need, if it is not a willing hand, we rob God — blunting some work that he would do through us.

Why should we be God's willing hands, helping to meet the needs of broken travelers on life's journey? Not because they are deserving (they may or may not be). The Samaritan didn't know whether the man in the ditch was deserving. Not because they are grateful (sometimes they are not). The Samaritan didn't know whether the man in the ditch would be grateful. Not because it's good social policy; not because it's tax deductible; not because it makes us "feel good" — but because we are part of the body of Christ, his hands and feet and lips and pocketbooks.

I am indebted to my friend, Dr. Kenneth Sauer, Bishop of the Southern Ohio Synod of The Evangelical Lutheran Church in America, for the following. During a severe flood in a midwestern community, the water had covered the streets several feet deep. A man was sitting on his porch, where the water was up to that level. Two men came by in a rowboat, pulled over to his porch and said, "Hop in, Brother, we'll take you to safety." He replied, "Not me, thanks, the *Lord* will help me."

The water continued to rise to the level of his porch roof, and he was perched up there. Two men came by in a motorboat. They pulled over to his porch roof and said, "Hop in, Brother, we'll take you to safety." He replied, "Not me, thank you. The *Lord* will help me."

The water rose to the roof of his house, and he was sitting up there when a helicopter came by. The pilot hovered above and let down a rope ladder. "Climb in, Brother, and we'll take you to safety." He answered, "Not me, thank you. The *Lord* will help me." The water continued to rise and the man drowned.

When he got to heaven, he spoke to the Lord. (How Bishops know what goes on up there I don't know.) The man said, "I've always gone to church, read my Bible, given my tithe, and said my prayers. There I was in great need of your help. Where were you when I needed you?" The Lord replied, "Where *was* I? I sent you two boats and a helicopter. What more do you want?"

The man had failed to realize that when God touches people he takes the nearest willing hand (or rowboat or helicopter) and uses that.

In the Samaritan story there is a subtle indictment of the institutional church. As is evident in his description of the priest and the Levite, as well as in other places, Jesus had no great admiration for the church leaders of his day. In his story he makes the one who was a real person, doing God's will, a Samaritan — a sort of halfbreed, upon whom Jesus' own race and institutional church looked down their noses.

In our day, the indictment against the institutional church has risen anew. The name and activity of "social ministry" is becoming part of every Christian congregation, insisting (and rightly so) that the organized church must not be simply a self-serving, self-perpetuating institution. Rather, it is to be a compassionate traveler on the road of life — a sort of corporate Good Samaritan. Wherever people are robbed of goods, well-being or the opportunity for a full life, there the church must be to champion their cause, to minister to their needs and to encourage their efforts. The church, like the Samaritan, must be willing to pay the cost — in cash, in caring, in whatever form is appropriate.

Most of this clamor today comes from within the church itself. Redirection and renewal are demands which the church is making of itself. Because this is so, in some places it has become the focal point of turmoil. To bind up the wounds of humanity on a collective scale, to improve the lot of whole *classes* of people faces us with many complications. It cuts across historical patterns, social structures and economic strata.

Not only is it costly in cash, it is unsettling to the emotions, disturbing to security and dynamite to the status quo. No wonder there is disagreement. On the one hand, there are people within the church who fear that the church of our day is irrelevant, not concerned enough with the plight of humanity. On the other hand, there are those (also within the church) who ask, "Why is the church concerned so much with social problems? Let the church stick to explaining the Bible and nurturing the spiritual life. Let the social problems be the concern of other agencies."

An emphasis on ministering to human need is long overdue in the institutional church. However, Jesus' story of the Good Samaritan reminds us of something that in all our arguments over mass programs, in all the frantic busyness of modern life, we are apt to forget: the need for personal daily kindness and compassion has not diminished.

We must not let our *zeal for* social programs take the place of our personal witnessing, nor let our *antagonism to* social programs poison our personal compassion. It's no use saying, "let them fend for themselves." The people who need us most are those who in one form or another have been beaten until they are no longer able — mentally, physically or financially — to fend for themselves.

The old principal is still the modern principal, and is relevant to our day, our society and our religion: when God touches people, he takes the nearest willing hand and uses that. When your heart's need is touched by the compassion, forgiveness or encouragement of another person; when your life is strengthened by the spiritual, mental or physical support of someone else, this is God, taking the nearest willing hand — or lips or purse — to express his love, his mercy, his concern for you.

Praise God when his modern Samaritans touch our lives, as they so often do. More important, praise God that *we* can be *(must be)* his Samaritans, touching life's needy travelers with our willing hands for him.

Almighty and most merciful God, help us to remember all those whom it is too easy to forget — the homeless, the destitute, the sick, the aged, and all those who have none to care for them. Prod us one by one as Christ's people, and together as Christ's body, the church, to remember Christ's nail torn wrists on the Cross, to be his willing hands today. Amen

16

Luke 10:38-42   *Proper 11 (C)*
                                  Pentecost 9 (L)
                              Ordinary Time 16 (RC)

Complaint from the Kitchen

A mother once told me that she wanted her daughter to be a complete Christian, so she named her Martha Mary. I have often wordered why she put the Martha first.

As we read the Gospel for today I sense an underlying sympathy for Martha in some of the housewives of the congregation. It just doesn't seem right, somehow, for one sister to be in the kitchen doing all the work of getting the meal while the other just sits and talks with the guest.

This sympathy is not limited to the housewives here today. I have only the initials (M.K.H., quoted in the *Salvation Army* magazine) of the person who wrote this verse, but I suspect that a lot of other initials could be added to it in spirit:

> *Lord of all pots and pans, since I've no time to be*
> *A saint by doing lovely things, or watching late with Thee*
> *Or dreaming in dawnlight, or storming heaven's gates*
> *Make me a saint by getting meals and washing up the plates.*

I suspect, too, that there are many men who share this sentiment, for whom Rudyard Kipling spoke when he wrote the following lines:

> *And the Sons of Mary smile and are blessed — they know*
> *   the angels are on their side.*
> *They know in them is the Grace confessed, and for them are*
> *   the Mercies multiplied.*

They sit at the Feet — they hear the Word — they see how truly the promise runs.
They have cast their burden upon the Lord and — the Lord he lays it on Martha's Sons!

Modern Christian Americans are mostly "doers." We place strong emphasis in the church on the idea that what counts is what we *do* for Jesus. Some would even go so far as to say that it doesn't matter so much what we *believe* — it's what we *do* that matters. Of course, that's somewhat like saying that it doesn't matter so much what the farmer *plants* — it's what he *reaps* that counts.

We read with a little reverent scepticism that our Lord tells Martha and us that Mary has "chosen the good portion." However, like all the words of Jesus, these words are sound and true — then and now — in the living of the Christian life. They are words that our fast-paced, often-frantic twentieth century needs to hear.

The coin of the Christian life has two sides: listening *to* Jesus and doing *for* Jesus. Jesus sets the priority in the Gospel for today.

Note first that worship is the central act of religion. A missionary was on a fast-paced journey to his station, with the assistance of some native baggage carriers. He was surprised one morning when they sat quietly in a circle and refused to move on. When he asked them why, they replied that they needed to let their souls catch up with their bodies.

A man assigned to the New York office of his company for a year went faithfully each Sunday to hear a famous New York preacher. He was surprised to hear him tell that same story twice within a few months. He said to the preacher, "That must be one of your favorite stories."

This was the reply: "I tell that story to the congregation twice a year. If there is anything a modern New Yorker needs to hear, it is something like that."

To sit at the feet of Jesus, to experience the joy of personal fellowship with Jesus, to sense the presence of our Lord is surely the richest privilege and the highest blessing of our faith. It floods the soul with joy and bathes the inward self with the refreshing streams of life. Worship is the central act of religion.

On his return from vacation, a pastor visited one of the elderly women of his congregation. He asked her what she thought of the sermons his substitute had preached. She said that they were helpful and refreshing. He asked her what the sermons were about and she told him she couldn't actually remember.

"Oh, my," the pastor said. "That's just as if you took this wicker basket down to the spring and filled it with water. By the time you got back there would be no water in it."

"That's true," she replied, "but the basket would be a whole lot cleaner."

How do we sing it? "Create in me a clean heart, O God, and renew a right spirit within me." (Psalm 51:10) This is what worship should do. To sit alone, or with others in the body of Christ, at the feet of Jesus — to sense his presence and hear his words, floods the soul with joy and bathes the inward self with the refreshing streams of life.

Or, to change the figure of speech, at worship the fires of the Christian life are lighted and fed. At worship we find and renew the reason for *and the inspiration to* live a life of Christian service to other people. Worship is the central act of religion.

Turn now to the other side of the coin of the Christian life — the relation of the exalted experience of worship to the mundane, practical life of Christian service. Listening *to* Jesus should issue in doing things *for* Jesus by loving and serving other people. We are not told whether Mary helped Martha with the after-dinner cleaning up when Jesus had gone, but we would hope that such a kindly, helpful relationship with her sister would be one result of sitting at the feet of Jesus.

There is a chapel somewhere in Wisconsin that has a stained glass window over the entrance, showing the figure of Jesus with open arms. Some, seeing it for the first time, remarked, "How meaningful! He seems to be inviting us in to worship."

"That's true," the pastor said. "He is indeed inviting us in to worship."

When the service was over and the same person was going out the door, he looked up at the window again. There was the figure of Jesus, with the same invitingly open arms. "Look!" he said. "Now he seems to be inviting us out."

"Right," the pastor replied. "The Jesus who invited you to worship now invites you out into the world to serve other people in his name."

Our Lord is greatly interested not only in what goes on in the church, but in what goes on in the office, the home and the factory. That's where people spend most of their time. That's where the Christian life is to be lived.

A mother, listening to the bedtime prayers of her small daughter, heard the listing of requests for blessings that children often offer — Mommy and Daddy and Grandma and Grandpa and on and on. She was surprised, however, to hear the child conclude her prayer with these words: "Now, Jesus, what would you like for me to do for *you*?"

The little girl had grasped the relationships of the Christian life: conversation of the heart (worship) *with* Jesus issues in the desire to do something *for* Jesus.

One of my radio listeners was inspired to write and send to me the following verse:

Dear God,
Each day,
When I come to pray
I ask so much of Thee.
In supplication
I bow
But seldom stay to see
What you might ask of me.
Today
Dear God,
When I come to pray

*Beseeching Thy love and care,
While I'm there
Give me courage
To stay and see
What you might ask of me!*

To be doers *of* the Word and witnesses *to* the Word is not only the fulfillment of our faith, but the mandate of the Master. Our Lord needs his Marys and his Marthas too.

The desire, the determination and the courage to serve our Lord comes from communion with him. The first priority of the Christian life is to sit at the feet of Jesus — absorbing through worship, Bible study and prayer what he is and what he teaches. All else follows that.

Our heavenly Father, grant that we may learn to love Jesus deeply and worship him. Amen

Luke 11:1-13

Proper 12 (C)
Pentecost 10 (L)
Ordinary Time 17 (RC)

The Sign in the Subway

On a subway platform in one of our Eastern states there was a large printed sign that said "God Answers Prayer." Some experienced person had scrawled across the bottom underneath the printed letters these words: "Sometimes the answer is NO!" This is what we have to deal with in any discussion of prayer.

Someone says, "I felt the need of God. I prayed for something to happen, and it didn't. Prayer failed." No, Sir. I suggest that you did not want God — you wanted God to *do* something, and that's different.

You have missed the purpose of prayer: to be in harmony with God, to have a sense of God's presence; to feel the assurance that God is in, around and greater than any circumstance; that, come what may, we belong to him and underneath are the everlasting arms. Prayer is not a trading post, but a line of communication.

Who needs lessons in prayer? Even the disciples did — and we do, too. The Gospel for today is one of Jesus' discussions on prayer. Let's see how he handles it.

At first these paragraphs seem disjointed, but they are not. They belong together. Verses one through four tell us what chiefly we should pray about. The other seven tell us what our attitude toward prayer should be.

We are to ask God to help us keep his name holy in our hearts and on our lips; to help us provide for our daily needs; to see the wisdom and necessity of forgiveness; to help us lead a life that is pleasing to him by strengthening us against temptation. The worst temptation of all is to doubt the wisdom and love of God.

Of course, Christians pray about other things — but Jesus here lifts up the main issues of the Christian life. Then, after teaching the major *contents* of prayer, beginning with verse five Jesus teaches us the attitude we should have toward prayer.

As was his custom, Jesus set his teaching in the form of a familiar experience. As his listeners knew, travel in that time and place was often done late in the day to avoid the heat. Hospitality, as they also knew, was an assumed necessity. Village bread was most often baked at home. The result of these things was the situation Jesus described, one which the disciples themselves might have shared on occasion. They could sympathize with the neighbor. To get out of a warm bed into the cold dark with no light and no fire was not pleasant: but still the neighbor's need was met. It was done "because of his importunity," Jesus said — his persistence in asking.

God is not a reluctant neighbor, but prayer that is sincere is persistent. Prayer is not wringing gifts from an unwilling God. It is talking with One who loves us beyond the love of an earthly father — One who sees the whole picture, who knows our needs better than we do, who does not meet them unless we ask with sincerity that shows itself in persistence.

Prayer is not a casual conversation, a quickie devotion, a flippant wish. It is a continuing dialogue between a person and God. Prayer is the soul's sincere desire, uttered or unexpressed. The original form of the words "ask, seek" used in this Gospel means "keep on asking, seeking." (Note that the householder was not asking for himself; he was asking for the welfare of his guests.)

This is not to say that one-time prayers are not sincere. But such prayers usually spring from fear or desperation in a critical situation. They are normally not a part of a "conversation of the believing heart with God," as the catechism defines prayer.

Sincere prayer involves persistence. Even *we* can sense insincerity. God, "unto whom all hearts are open," *always* knows. The youthful Augustine prayer, "O God, make me pure, but not yet." A man once prayed, "O Lord, help my mother-in-law — but I don't insist on it." Of course, much of our insincerity is not that obvious.

A man once said that his life and faith were strengthened mightily when one night he opened his mother's bedroom door and saw her on her knees in prayer. He said, "I heard her mentioning my name to the Lord, asking that he would guide me to be strong against temptation and to lead a life that was pleasing in his sight. I realized, then, that she had been doing this every night of my life. I have not been the same since that night." This is persistent prayer.

If a reluctant neighbor can be pressed into giving his neighbor what he needs, how much more will God, who is a loving father, supply his children's needs? Why, then, some will ask, does God not always give me what I persistently pray for?

God gives what is best for our ultimate good. "What father among you, if his son asks for a fish, will instead of a fish give him a snake?" But what if a son, not aware of the danger in snakes, asks for a snake? Will a loving father give him that? Neither will God. Sometimes, as Jesus once said to the mother of James and John, the sons of Zebedee, we do not know what we ask. (Matthew 20:22) No matter how convinced and insistent we are that we know best, God's answer must be "No."

Saint Augustine was a wild and profligate youth. His mother prayed for him constantly. The early chapters of the *Confessions* of Saint Augustine are filled with references to his mother's earnest prayers that he might become a Christian. One day he told her he was going to Italy with some companions. She believed that if he went to that sinful city there would be no hope of his reform.

She prayed earnestly that God would not allow him to go to Italy. She did all she could to prevent it, even so far as to follow him on the early part of the journey, until he tricked her and went on with the journey. It was in Milan that he came under the influence of Saint Ambrose and put his reluctant feet on the first step of the ladder that led to baptism, to Holy Orders and to sainthood. His mother's ultimate prayers for him were answered in the very place that her present prayers asked God never to allow him to go.

About the turn of the century J. J. Wagner wrote a spine-tingling story about a mother and father who were granted three wishes through the "tragic magic" of a monkey's paw. They wished first for two hundred pounds. That evening they were brought word that their son had been killed and partly mutilated by a machine in a horrible accident where he worked. The company was compensating them with two hundred pounds.

In grief and panic the mother used the second wish — that they might have their son back. In the middle of that night there came a groaning and a rattling sound as if someone were dragging himself across their front porch in the dark; then a repeated knocking on the front door. The father feared the truth — the mangled body of their son. Immediately he used the third wish — that the ghoulish corpse would disappear. How better it would have been if the first answer had been "No."

Sincere prayer is not the rubbing of a monkey's paw — but the story makes a point. Sometimes we know not what we ask, and do not see the possible consequences of our prayers, so a loving father has to answer "No."

Sincere prayer not only involves persistence; it also involves commitment. Our actions must be suited to and undergird our prayers. For instance, if we set a bad example for our children, how can we expect God to answer "Yes" to our prayers to make them good? Our actions are working against our prayers. Our inner life of prayer and our outer life of activity must be suited to and undergird each other.

Above all, we need to trust God that he *is* a loving father, that he sees the whole picture and cares for our ultimate good.

Granted, sometimes it is not easy when we think in our restricted vision that what we ask in our prayers is the way things ought to be.

"If you, then, who are evil," Jesus said, "know how to give good gifts to your children, how much more will the heavenly Father give . . ." The fur coat? The healthiest body in the block? The winning points in the game? The million dollar deal? No, that's not what Jesus said, is it? He said "How much more will the heavenly Father give the Holy Spirit to them that ask him."

God's supreme gift is the gift of the Holy Spirit. What does the Holy Spirit do? She prompts us to continual conversation with God. She directs our energies in the direction of our prayers. She keeps us sensitive to the signs God gives to change direction and ideas. She keeps us assured of God's love, so that when the answer is "No," we are sure it is for the ultimate good of ourselves and of those for whom we pray. The following lines should help us keep our prayers in the proper perspective:

I asked God for strength that I might achieve;
I was made weak that I might learn humbly to obey.

I asked for health that I might do great things;
I was given infirmity that I might do better things.

I asked for riches that I might be happy;
I was given poverty that I might be wise.

I asked for all things that I might enjoy life;
I was given life that I might enjoy all things.

I got nothing that I asked for but everything I had hoped for;
Despite myself, my prayers were answered. I am, among all people, most richly blessed.

No one sermon, no one Bible passage can completely explain all the nuances of our relationship with God in prayer, but the teaching of this Gospel passage is clear: these are things we are to chiefly pray about, and this is the attitude we are to have in prayer.

> *Our heavenly Father, help us to remember always that you love us and care about us; that you know not only the prayers of our lips, but the deeper prayers that are hidden in our hearts. Help us to trust that however you answer our prayers, the answer is for our ultimate good — that in your will is our peace. In Jesus' name. Amen*

Luke 12:13-21 *Proper 13 (C)*
Pentecost 11 (L)
Ordinary Time 18 (RC)

The Foolish Farmer

Note, first, that God did not say this man was evil. God said he was a fool.

Note, secondly, that most of *us* would not say he was a fool. We'd say he was an obviously successful businessman. We esteem abundance. Jesus said, "A man's life does not consist in the abundance of his possessions." We act as though a man's life *does* consist in the abundance of his possessions. We have a saying, "If you're so smart, why aren't you rich?". As if *that* were the test of a person's life.

Why would God call him a fool? It was not because he saved. Jesus saved even the fragments of a picnic lunch, that nothing be lost.

It was not because he was wealthy. The monastery notwithstanding, poverty is not the requirement nor the guarantee of heaven. The one whom we have called the "rich young ruler" was told to sell all that he had because *that* was the barrier that kept him from following Jesus. God called this man a fool not because of his wealth, but because of his attitude toward wealth.

Someone asked John D. Rockefeller (of all people) "How much wealth does it take to satisfy a person?" He replied, "Just a little bit more." The Romans had a proverb: "Money is like sea water; the more you drink, the thirstier you become."

Why would God call this man a fool? I once heard the late, great Oscar Blackwelder name four reasons. Let me list them for you (with commentary).

1. *He left God out of his gratitude.*
He said plenty about himself, but nothing about God. In his prosperity parade he was in the reviewing stand alone. *His* goods, *his* fruits, *his* barns. God? Not the first thought. *His* planning, *his* brains, *his* work, *his* genius. There is not even the mention of God's name. There are sixty-one words in this procession of abundance; twelve of them are the first person singular: *my*.

A grand Christian man once said, "It is not how much of my possessions I use for God; it is how much of God's possessions I keep for myself."

Recall the nursery rhyme:

Little Jack Horner sat in a corner
Eating his Christmas pie.
He stuck in his thumb
And pulled out a plumb
And said [of all the ridiculous things to say!]
"What a good boy am I."

Not "What a good farmer my father is." Not "What a good cook my mother is." No. "What a good boy am I." The man in this Gospel text could have modeled for that rhyme.

A teacher was talking to a class of little boys about the presence of God in daily life. He asked them if God is everywhere, and they correctly answered, "Yes." In an effort to get the matter closer to their own personal living, he named actual situations. Is God in the church? Yes. Is God in the home? Yes. On the street? Yes. Is God in the city prison? Silence. That one had them stopped. Finally one boy came up with as good an answer as I've heard. "Yes, God is there, but those fellows don't know it."

That was this man's trouble, wasn't it? God was in his life, but he didn't know it. God was in his fruits, God was in his fields, God was in his goods. God was everywhere except in his gratitude.

2. *He left other people out of his possessions.*
As a nation, we come perilously close to this ourselves. What shall America, beautiful for spacious skies, do with its amber waves of grain? Ship it to the hungry of the world? Evidently not much — for that, we are told, would disrupt the economic structure and cause international problems across the world.

We draw perilously near this foolish farmer, also, in our obsession with material things. It is too easy to become content with what ministers to the body — food, clothes, fine surroundings, and all the gadgets of convenience that make life easy. These things can become ends in themselves and insulate a person from what is happening around him and within him. This obsession with material things can wither our sympathy and blind us to other people's needs. A concentration on material things can close us in on ourselves until we become first cousin to the farmer in the parable.

In his book *The Compassionate Christ*, Walter Russel Bowie quotes an unknown author who penned these lines:

He used his health
To store up wealth
To get, to scrimp and save.
Then spent his wealth
To get back health
And only got a grave.

3. *He left his soul out of his thoughts.*
This often happens when we put material things first, and make them the center of life, as this man did. How much thought do *we* give to the soul — that intangible, unknowable entity which separates us from the animals? It is the only eternal part of our otherwise temporal nature, but our daily doings often seem more urgent and important.

His higher nature had evidently not been fed at the table of the Lord, so he and God were worlds apart. They weren't speaking the same language at all. He said, "My goods." God said, "Your soul." When it is a choice between goods and God, which do we choose?

Here is the line of demarcation between what we have and what we are: what we have we must leave behind; what we are we must keep forever. "Then whose will these goods be?" Jesus asked. Always there is the *then whose* in our life. What we have we leave; what we are we must keep forever.

The governor of one of our States was making a tour of its institutions. While he was touring a home for the mentally retarded he saw one woman working industriously at an old-fashioned sewing machine. "Is that one of the inmates?" he asked. "Yes." "I see no reason for her to be here using the taxpayer's money. Why can't she be released?"

He watched the woman for a few minutes. She worked on, never pausing for a moment to rest. She pumped the lever with her foot. She pushed the cloth through the machine with her hands, watching intently and carefully with her eyes. "I order this woman examined for release." Then he looked again. Pumping hard with her feet, pushing the cloth with her hands, watching intently with her eyes — but there was no thread in the needle.

Industrious? Yes. Hard work? Yes — plenty. Goods enough and to spare, but nothing to hold them together and make them meaningful. What are goods and industry if the thread that makes them meaningful is missing? Goods, goods, goods, — pumping, working — to have at last just goods that are never used to make the wedding garment that fits us for the bridegroom's chamber. Goods — grasping, envying, coveting goods — will leave us at last with full hands and an empty soul.

The farmer said, "My goods." God said, "Your soul." He said, "Soul, thou has much goods," and God said, "You fool!"

4. *He left eternity out of his plans.*
He said, "For many years." God said, "Tonight." He thought that because he had his goods in one hand he had the future in the other; but God said, "Tonight."

One of my wise seminary professors told us to remember

when we stepped into the pulpit that someone there may be hearing the Gospel for the first time, and someone hearing it for the last time. Over the years, many times someone in the church that Sunday has been in the cemetery before the next Sunday comes.

We like to think that life is predictable, and sometimes it is. Like this man, it is our nature to plan for many years; but still we say, "A bird in the hand is worth two in the bush." Heaven is at the end of a heartbeat, and eternity is but one breath away. He left eternity out of his plans. He planned for the probable — many years. He neglected the inevitable, when God says, "Tonight."

He said, "My goods — my goods, for many years." God said, "You fool — your soul — tonight." We would endow him with respectability and call him a success. God endowed him with death and called him a fool.

I have a disturbing thought every time I read about this man. Maybe you are having it, too. How very much he looks like me? I don't have bursting barns — but how often in my stupid conceit have I left God out of my gratitude? How often in my grasping selfishness have I left other people out of my possessions? There are times when I think much about my goods and little about my soul; when I have planned carefully for next week, and carelessly for eternity. It is a staggering thought, and it drives me to my knees and makes me exclaim, "God have mercy on me — a fool."

Our heavenly Father, help us to take an honest look at ourselves — to try to see ourselves as you see us. Save us from being fools like this man. Amen

Luke 12:32-40 (C, L)
Luke 12:32-48 (RC)

Proper 14 (C)
Pentecost 12 (L)
Ordinary Time 19 (RC)

The Emperor's Son-in-law

This Gospel hinges on responsibility, and the culmination of it is in verse forty-eight: "Everyone to whom much is given, of him shall much be required."

One of the favorite stories of the great Danish philosopher, Soren Kierkegard, concerns an emperor, touring his domain and receiving the accolades of his people. When the entourage reached the market square of one village, his carriage was surrounded by cheering villagers and peasants. To the amazement of his neighbors, one brash young farmer stepped out of the crowd and approached the emperor's carriage.

"Give me a boon, Sire," he pleaded. "Grant me a special blessing."

The villagers were even more amazed at the emperor's reply: "Of course, my good man," he said. "Get into my carriage. Come with me. Live in my palace. Eat at my table. Marry my daughter. Be my son-in-law."

The young man exclaimed his delight. To be the emperor's son-in-law! Then he thought about it. No more Saturday nights at the pub with his friends. No more dirty, comfortable peasant clothes. He'd have to get dressed up. He'd have to take a bath — maybe every week. He'd have to clean his fingernails. He'd have to learn the manners of the court.

He sadly shook his head and lowered his eyes. "No, Sire," he said. "I would be too uncomfortable. It would pull me out of my comfortable customs. It would be too hard to live up to. It would take too much of me."

"If you want to do something for me, give me a plot of ground, a farm, a house of my own; but to live in your palace, eat at your table, be your son-in-law — this is too much." So he declined it.

You see — he wanted the emperor's blessing; but he wanted it on his own terms. He wanted to be blessed in doing what *he* wanted to do — not what *the emperor* wanted him to do. He wanted to be blessed right where he was, not moved out of his comfortable customs. He wanted the blessing, but not the responsibility that went with it.

Too often *we* are that peasant. The Bible says many wonderful things about us Christians. Paul says, "We are the children of God; if children, then heirs — heirs of God and fellow heirs with Christ. (Romans 8:16-17) In 1 Peter 2:9 we are told, "You are a royal priesthood, God's own people, that you may declare the wonderful works of him who called you out of darkness into his marvelous light."

Peter goes on to remind us Christians in his second letter, "His divine power has granted to us all things that pertain to life and godliness, through the knowledge of him who called us to his own glory and excellence, by which he has granted to us his precious and very great promises, that through these you may . . . become partakers of the divine nature." (2 Peter 1:3-4)

Blessings, indeed! And as Christians we lay claim to them. Then in, through and under them is the story of the Steward. It ends with the demanding words of Jesus, words from which we shrink in our self-centered daily life: "To whom much is given, of him will much be required."

Peter says more about our blessings as the people of God: "For this very reason make every effort to supplement your faith with virtue, and virtue with knowledge, and knowledge with self-control, and self-control with steadfastness, and steadfastness with godliness, and godliness with brotherly affection, and brotherly affection with love." (2 Peter 1:5-7)

This business about being God's children — heirs of God

with Christ — sounds great. But to be expected to live up to it is sometimes more then we bargain for. To be God's children — to be his royal priesthood — is to be those to whom much is given. But to be those from whom much is expected is something else again. Yet that's what this business of being a Christian is all about — accepting the stewardship responsibility of being Christ's redeemed people.

Too often we seek God's blessing on our terms. We choose what we want to do, and ask God to bless it. But to ask what *he* wants *us* to do leads to all kinds of inconvenience. This is behind much false humility that most pastors hear from time to time: "I'm afraid." Translation: "Don't expect much commitment out of me, brother, because you're not going to get it."

Or this one: "I'm a Christian in my own small way, but I like to stay in the background." Translation: "I want to be known as a child of God, but I don't want to do much to serve my Lord." When such people are asked to take some responsibility in the Lord's work they answer, "Oh, I'm *sure* you can find *someone* who is much more capable than I am." Translation: "I want to be a child of God, but I don't want any of the responsibility that goes with it. I'll take the promises, but not the tasks."

Too often we, like the peasant, want to be one to whom much is given, but not one from whom much is expected. The problem is that this is not the cheap blessing God offers — which is why some people get discouraged with God, with prayer and with religion. God calls us to eat at his table, to be one of his family, to accept the responsibility of being his sons and daughters. God gives us his blessings through (that is, by means of) our commitment.

One day I met a stranger on a public tennis court and played some tennis with him. When we finished, I complimented him on his game. "Well," he said, "it's not as good as it used to be. We're visiting relatives here in your city. I'm just getting into my game again. We've just returned from three years in the mission field in Africa, and they didn't have tennis courts there."

"Are you a minister?" I asked. "No."
"A doctor?" "No." "A dentist?" "No."
"Then what are you?" "I'm a carpenter."
"What did you do there?"

"I built an infirmary, a small hangar for the mission plane and a couple of small houses."

This was his story: "We've always gone to church and loved the Lord. I've always prayed 'Lord, use me as you will — but after all, I'm only a humble carpenter.' One night when I was at the church serving refreshments to the Men's Brotherhood I got a phone call from our national headquarters. 'John, we want you to take your wife and two children to the mission field in Africa for three years.' My wife and I talked it over and prayed about it, and we decided it was either put up or shut up. So we went."

I was fascinated. I asked, "How did it work out?"

This was his reply: "They were the three happiest years our family has ever spent together."

God gives his blessings through our commitment to his will. God is abundant with his blessings, but high in his expectations. We want to be the children of God, but are we ready for the commitment of being his children? Do we *really* want God's blessing of invitation: "Come, be in my family, eat at my table"? To whom much is given, from them shall much be required.

There's nothing wrong with talking to God about better beans or bigger cabbages in whatever peasant gardens we happen to till. There's nothing wrong with talking to God about a pay raise or a healthy body or a happy home life. But if that's *all* we want, if that's the only boon we seek — "Bless me in my rut, make it comfortable, and by all means make it profitable, but don't push me out of it and ask me to do things that are inconvenient for me." — we had better read our Bibles again. God gives his blessings through our commitment to his will.

How did the carpenter put it? "Three of the happiest years

our family has ever spent together." We ask for little blessings not in humility, but because we are afraid of the big ones God might offer if we seek his will. God offers the big one. Accept the responsibility of being members of his family and do what is needed. The little blessings cling to that along the way, like iron filings to a magnet.

A pastor came to his new congregation and preached his first sermon on commitment. He talked about tithing, about teaching Sunday church school, about witnessing for the Lord among neighbors and friends. The congregation complimented him on his sermon. "That's fine, Pastor," they said. We needed to hear that."

The peasant said, "No, Sire," and declined it. The carpenter said it was either put up or shut up. What do we say? The third Sunday he preached the same sermon. Nobody said much going out the door, but the elders took him off in a corner and asked with as much patience as they could muster, "Pastor, don't you have another one, maybe, that we could hear?"

"*Another* one?" he asked. "Why, you haven't done anything about the first one yet. When you do, then we'll talk about another one."

I don't recommend doing that, but the pastor has a point.

God expects our tithe, be it great or small. When we are asked to help with the Lord's work, he expects us to say "Yes." We are those to whom much is given. Christ has bought us and paid for us on the holy Cross. He has done for us what we could not do for ourselves nor for each other. He has loved us and redeemed us and opened the gates of God's heart and home.

To whom much is given, of them shall much be required. Ours is the responsibility of being willing and faithful stewards in the Master's household. We are the children of God. Ours is the commitment that comes with being members of his royal family.

The peasant said, "No, Sire," and declined it. The carpenter said it was either put up or shut up. What do we say?

Luke 12:49-56 (C)
Luke 12:49-53 (L, RC)

Proper 15 (C)
Pentecost 13 (L)
Ordinary Time 20 (RC)

Our Splintered World

We live in a splintered world. Each week *Time* magazine has a section on "The World" — revealing revolution, apartheid, violence and cruelty, along with occasional good news. There is also a section on "The Nation," frequently revealing these same things closer to home.

There is evidence of splintered families all around us and among us. A cartoon strip showed a young woman talking to a minister. She said, "John and I are having a terrible time, and we need your advice. We are trying to decide how to divide the furniture, who gets what of the money we've saved and who gets custody of the children."

"Oh," the minister asked, "are you contemplating divorce?"

"Oh, no," she replied. "We are trying to work out our *prenuptial agreement.*"

There are devout Christian parents who, as far as they know, have tried to maintain a Christian home and serve as attractive Christian examples. However, one of their sons or daughters turns away from Jesus — to evil companions, to dope or theft and all the heartache those things bring. Such parents can only sorrowfully ask, "Where did we go wrong?" and pray and love the prodigal in the hope that the husks of the far country will bring the child at last to himself and to the Father's home again.

A splintered world, indeed!

At Jesus's birth the angels sang, "Peace on earth and goodwill to men." It comes as somewhat of a shock, then, to worshiping Christians to be reminded by Jesus himself, as we are in the Gospel for today, that the world was then and is now splintered over Jesus.

"Do you think that I have come to give peace on the earth? No, I tell you, but rather division." Jesus lived in the real world. He saw, with sorrow and compassion, the sunlight and the shadows of human nature. He did not delude himself that he would be universally accepted. Our world, from ancient Palestine to modern America, is evidence of the clarity of his vision.

What are the divisions regarding Jesus? There are, of course, those who love him, follow him and serve him: Peter, Paul, Joan of Arc, Wilfred Grenfell, Mother Teresa and a host of others — some of whom are here today.

Then there are those who try to be neutral toward him; like Pilate, who said, "I find no fault in this just person — but see you to it" (Matthew 27:24); like Nicodemus, who came to Jesus by night and called him "a teacher come from God" and got a sermon on commitment for his trouble (John 3:2); like some moderns who try to say that Jesus is a good man — but only that and nothing more.

Neutrality toward Jesus is not possible, as Pilate discovered. Every person must come down on one side or the other. Jesus said, "He who is not with me is against me." (Matthew 12:30) He cannot be "just a good man." Either he is God as he claimed to be — "I and the Father are one" (John 10:30) and "He that has seen me has seen the Father" (John 14:9) — or else he is not even a good man, but one of the most audacious liars and first-class frauds that history has produced. No matter how we try to delude ourselves in the attempt, there can be no neutrality toward Jesus. Every person must come down on one side or the other.

Then there are those who despise and reject him — from the Pharisees who engineered his crucifixion to the Turks who ravaged his homeland to modern anti-Christian nations, groups and persons.

I have a picture that pinpoints the early division over Jesus. It is a crude cartoon of a jackass on a cross, and under it are the words "Alexamenes worships his God."

Today Christian churches, once open to every passer-by, are being kept locked because they are being vandalized and looted with a vicious contempt — a modern version of the division over Jesus, an updating of the ancient contempt "Alexamenes worships his God."

Jesus said, "I came to bring division." The important question for us is this: Where are we in this division? How does this Gospel apply to us? At least three things apply.

1. Since we are here at worship, of course we assume that we are those who love and serve him. This is devoutly to be hoped, but we need to examine our attitudes to see how true it is. Are we being faithful in our witness for him? Or is our sometimes-polite silence a facade for a flabby neutrality? Is our occasional church attendance only a sop to social conformity? Is our anemic stewardship only a salve for an uncommitted life?

A wife and her small son visited our church, so I called in their home one evening that week. Only the husband, whom I had not met, was at home. We talked about church, and he said he guessed he was a member somewhere "back home" but he wasn't sure. Then he added "My wife is the church-goer in our family."

I asked him as kindly as I could, "As far as Christianity is concerned, whose side are you on?"

He laughed and said, "I guess I'm not on anybody's side, as you put it." But he was! Not to decide is to decide.

How different from the totally-deaf man who went to church faithfully every Sunday. There was no interpretation in sign language, and he couldn't hear a word that was said or sung. One day one of his "non-church" acquaintances wrote him a note asking why he went to church all the time when he couldn't hear anything. The deaf man replied, "I don't want there to be any doubt about which side I'm on."

Can there be any doubt as to which side *you* are on?

2. We cannot force the Christian life on others, but if we are true to our witness for Jesus we can do our best to exhibit it and make it attractive to others. Our witness is not to condemn, but to invite — to tell in words and show in deeds what Jesus means to us; to tell and show with kindly conviction the strengthening power of our prayer and Bible study, and let the Holy Spirit use it as he will.

A man came to church and asked for instruction as to how to become a member. He said, "A friend of mine has a joy and strength in his life that I sorely need in mine. He says he gets it here. I need the Lord that he has." Are people attracted to Christ by what they see in us and hear from us?

3. If we are true to our witness for Jesus, there will be opposition, just as there was to our Lord himself. We can expect it. No one is asking for our crucifixion, but there are those who will call us "goody-two-shoes" and ridicule our Christian faith as "pie-in-the-sky-bye-and-bye." Our daily life should show that it is not "pie-in-the-sky-bye-and-bye" but the "drum and fife in the strife and life," and that's different.

A jokingly contemptuous man once said to a pastor, "I use the same words on the golf course that you do in church, except in a different setting." It was more than a different setting, of course — a different attitude, a different way of life, a different side of the division which Jesus described.

The exclamation, "Jesus Christ!" can be either a devotion or an epithet, but it can't be both. Neutrality toward Jesus is impossible, attempt it as some people may.

Jesus said, "Do you think I have come to give peace on earth? No, I tell you, but rather division." When Abraham Lincoln was first introduced to Harriet Beecher Stowe, who wrote *Uncle Tom's Cabin*, he said, "So this is the little lady who started the Civil War." However true that incident may be, she wrote not to bring peace, but division, and people had to decide where they stood.

> *There was a knight of Bethlehem*
> *Whose wealth was tears and sorrows*
> *His men at arms were little lambs*
> *His trumpeters were sparrows*
> *His castle was a wooden cross*
> *On which he hung so high*
> *His helmet was a crown of thorns*
> *Whose crest did touch the sky.*
>
> — *Author unknown*

This is the man that brought the judgment of God upon the people. This is the man that divides families, communities and nations. The division he brought extends from his day to our day, and each person must decide which side he or she is on. There is no neutrality. "He who is not with me is against me." (Matthew 12:30)

So it comes right down to the personal question: in the division over Jesus, which side are *you* on? How does *your* witness, *your* way of life, *your* stewardship of time and talent answer that question?

Luke 13:22-30

Proper 16 (C)
Pentecost 14 (L)
Ordinary Time 21 (RC)

The Turnstile at the Pearly Gate

Have you ever been among the great crowd moving toward the entrance to a big time football game? At first the entrance seems wide and open to all; but once you begin seriously pushing and struggling to go in you discover that the gate is not wide at all. The broad gate narrows down to a turnstile where you enter one by one, and the keeper says, "Hold your own ticket, please."

So Jesus describes the door to the Kingdom. It begins wide and open to all — but then comes the struggle to go through the narrow door: one at a time, and hold your own ticket.

I

This does not match up with our sometimes comfortable idea of the Christian life: being king when it's not too difficult; going to worship when it's convenient; giving a little money when it's tax deductible; helping with the Lord's work when we feel like it; acknowledging Jesus as Savior when we happen to think about it.

It's easy to think that once we are members of the church we have reached the goal, come to the end of the road, and our striving for the Kingdom of God is done. One man was in a congregation that was singing Reginald Heber's great hymn, "The Son of God goes forth to war." The last line of that hymn says: "O God, to us may grace be given to follow in their train." He was surprised to hear the woman standing next to him sing: "O God, to us may grace be given to follow *on the train.*"

The Christian life is a constant striving to do the will of God as Jesus revealed it. The Christian life is not simply a destination, but a journey.

Jesus says we are to "strive to enter the narrow door." It is interesting to note that the Greek word for "strive" is the same word from which we get our word "agony." "Will those who are saved be few?" they asked. His reply says, in effect, that we are not to worry about that, but the door is narrow and we are to strive to enter by that narrow door.

II

We are to *strive* ("agonize") to enter. That seems like a strong word for the kingdom of a loving God. We should not be too surprised: there are many narrow doors in our life where those who enter must strive to enter. It is true of the scholar who, in Milton's words, must "scorn delights and live laborious days." It is true of the athlete, who must scorn rich food, engage in rigid discipline and practice with constant, faithful diligence. It is true of the musician.

Someone once said to Paderewski, the great pianist, "Sir, you are a genius."

He replied, "Madam, before I was a genius I was a drudge." He said that if he missed practice one day, he noticed it; if he missed practice two days, the critics noticed it; if he missed three days, his family noticed it; if he missed four days, the audience noticed it. The door is narrow. Why should we think we can "drift" into the Kingdom of God?

It is reported that after one of Fritz Kreisler's concerts a young woman said to him, "I would give my life to be able to play like that."

He replied, "That's what I gave."

The Christian life is a constant striving to do the will of

God as Jesus revealed it. Why this need to *strive*? Because there are forces of evil within us trying to pull us down. Have you ever tried to walk up a down escalator? Not to strive upward is to be constantly pulled down. There are forces of evil within us and around us, constantly trying to pull us down from generosity to selfishness; from compassion to indifference; from sacrifice to greed.

A little boy once asked his mother if people who told lies went to heaven. She replied (perhaps unwisely) "Of course not."

"Well," he said, "it must be awfully lonesome there with only God and George Washington." Of course. So "lie a little," the forces of evil say. "Why struggle with it? Be partially honest, relatively pure, occasionally forgiving, comparatively loving, sometimes reverent. Relax. Nobody's perfect."

III

Each of us must enter on our own — not because we ate and drank where he happened to be; not because he taught on our street. Each one is to strive to enter the Kingdom. We enter in not because we go to church suppers; not because there's a church on our street. Each one must strive to enter the Kingdom on our own.

A man does not enter the Kingdom because his wife is a member of the church women's society. A woman does not enter the Kingdom because her cousin is a missionary. Each must strive to enter on our own.

There are times, of course, when our striving seems useless. The goal of Christian living is unattainable, impossible; but that is not the point. The point is: are we doing all we can? An ancient king once built a temple to God. His name was on the entrance wall as the prime mover of the project. However, above his name on the wall he placed the name of an unknown woman. After her name were the words, "She has done what she could. After work was done each day, in compassion she gathered the hay to feed the oxen." Obscure heroes will be found at the judgment — those who have done what they could.

In one of the youth hymnals there is a hymn whose first verse reads:

> *Living for Jesus a life that is true*
> *Striving to please him in all that I do;*
> *Yielding allegiance, glad hearted and free*
> *This is the pathway of blessing for me.*

Striving!

Here, of course, the New Testament teaching of Justification by Faith comes in. We are made acceptable to God by our personal faith in Jesus as our Savior; by our own public profession of Jesus as our Savior. Martin Luther, in his great hymn "Ein' Feste Burg," wrote

> *Were not the right man on our side*
> *Our striving would be losing.*

We are not saved by works, but by grace through faith alone; yet if this faith *in* Jesus — this profession *of* Jesus as our Savior — is genuine, it will have a constant meaning for our daily living. It is not that we must do good works to be redeemed. We don't do good works for Jesus in order to be saved; we do good works for Jesus as the outward sign that we *are* saved. They are the outward evidence of our inward faith.

Do you love the Lord? The opposite of love is not hate — it is indifference. Lots of people don't actively hate Jesus and what he taught; they are simply indifferent to it, doing what suits *them*, not what suits *him*.

IV

It is God's judgment, not the world's, that will determine the citizens of the Kingdom. Someone once said to a woman,

"Your husband seems like a wonderful man." Out of her years of intimate experience she replied, "You don't have to live with him."

Intimate experience, not outward appearances, determines what we really are. God lives intimately with us. He knows our thoughts, our ambitions, our desires. He is the one, as the confessional service puts it, "to whom all hearts are open, all desires known and from whom no secrets are hid." What will *his* judgment be? Never mind what the neighbors think.

Jesus points out that for each of us the time is short. "When once the householder has risen up and shut the door, you will begin to stand outside and knock at the door, saying 'Lord, open to us.' He will answer you, 'I do not know where you come from.' " There will come a day — we know not how soon — when God will say to us, as Jesus told the farmer in Luke 12:20, "This night your soul will be required of you."

In this Gospel Jesus is telling us that the Christian faith is an active, lifelong striving, with God's help, against the evil in ourselves and in our world. The end of it is a narrow door where we enter — *if* we enter — like a turnstile: one at a time, holding our own ticket.

Our heavenly Father, inspire us with your Holy Spirit, that we shall not be listless and do-less in our faith, but eager, determined to do our utmost for the Lord Jesus our Savior. Amen

Luke 14:1, 7-14 *Proper 17 (C)*
Pentecost 15 (L)
Ordinary Time 22 (RC)

The Man Who Came to Dinner

To the thoughtful reader of this Gospel two questions jump out at once: Why was Jesus invited to a dinner with the Pharisees on the Sabbath? And why did he accept? In answer to that, there are three key sentences in this Gospel, and all three come across the centuries and speak Jesus' word to us.

I

"They were watching him." (verse 1) Lo! Our two questions are answered. He was invited so they could watch him. What further evidence could they gather to feed the fire of their animosity toward him? Obviously he knew they were watching him, so he gave them ample evidence as to the kind of person he was. In verse twenty-six, for example, which is omitted from our reading, a man with dropsy was planted in his path. Would he break their law by healing on the Sabbath? He would, and he did.

This was no happy social occasion. They watched him, and he gave them plenty to see and to hear. Jesus had the moral courage not to be intimidated by their opposition; not to bend his principles and camouflage his character because the host and guests did not agree with him. The implication for us is obvious. How often do our Christian convictions and our moral standards bow down to social politeness, economic advantage or manifest disagreement? Do people know where we stand?

II

"For everyone who exalts himself will be humbled and he who humbles himself will be exalted." (verse 11)

In spite of its underlying truth, many of them did not believe it, and many of us don't either. We have a saying that carries much more weight with us: "He that tooteth not his own horn, verily it shall not be tooted."

Saint Augustine stressed three basic Christian principles: the first is humility, the second is humility and the third is humility. But Leo Durocher said, "Nice guys finish last." That is more to our way of thinking.

Yet, underneath, we know that the verdict of Jesus is sound. "The world," we say, "accepts your estimate of yourself"; but that is often not true either. Self-confidence is not conceit, but it can easily become conceit if it is not bridled and controlled. Most of us at times encounter people who "think more highly of themselves than they ought to think," as Paul wrote to the Romans. (Romans 12:3) We sense that they are more to be pitied than envied — cardboard figures who soon or late are humbly brought from the clouds of delusion back to earth by the hard facts of life.

Status questions often arose in Jesus' day, just as they do in our day. For example, how often have we heard nasty remarks and hurt feelings over who should sit in what pew at the wedding and who should sit near the bride and groom at the wedding dinner?

Of course, there is a false humility that repels us because we recognize it as only another form of conceit. A man said, "I used to be conceited, egotistical and unbearable to people. Nobody liked me. But now I'm the most modest, likeable guy you ever met, and everybody likes me."*

---

* It is interesting to note that such diverse writers as Samuel Taylor Coleridge (1771-1834) and Robert Southey (1774-1843) both claim that the Devil's favorite sin is "pride that apes humility."

> *And the Devil did grin, for his darling sin*
> *Is pride that apes humility.* Coleridge, The Devil's Thoughts
> *The Devil owned with a grin that his favorite*
> *Is pride that apes humility.* Southey, The Devil's Walk

There is much to keep us humble if we have the sense to see it. We compare ourselves to the experts in any line of work or sport rather than to our inferiors. In moral and spiritual things we can compare ourselves to Jesus rather than to one another or to the person down the street. Or, we can remember what we owe to others who led us, nourished us and corrected us along the way. As Paul said, "I am debtor both to the Greeks and to the Barbarians; both to the wise and the unwise." (Romans 1:14) Above all, we can remember what we owe to the Lord.

A man had a gold-plated safety pin which he carried in his pocket. Frequently he would be seen fingering it. Someone asked him one day what the significance of the pin was. He told, in answer, how he had run away from a fine home, mixed with the wrong crowd, gone from one trouble to another, finally ending in poverty and degradation. He had sold his overcoat to get money for liquor, and on a cold winter night he had his sweater pinned together with that safety pin. He walked into a mission to keep warm, and there the Lord Jesus Christ found him. After he came to know the Lord he started a new life. It brought him many successes and material possessions. He had that pin gold plated to remind him of what he once had been before he knew the Lord. The feel of that pin forever robbed him of any thoughts of pride or conceit over what he had accomplished. His own strength had left him desolate and dissolute. He knew what the redemptive grace of Jesus had done.

For most of us it is not that drastic or dramatic, but fortunate are those who have some form or version of the gold-plated safety pin to keep them humble in success. True humility is not weakness — it is strength. True humility is not cowardice — it is courage. It is strength and courage to be grateful, not supercilious, for what we are, what we can do, what we have done; courage and strength to recognize and remember "that a power not our own" has had a hand in it all.

III

"But when you give a dinner or a banquet, do not invite your friends or your brothers or your kinsmen or rich neighbors, lest they invite you in return, and you be repaid. Invite the poor, the maimed, the lame and blind and you will be blessed because they cannot repay you." (verse 14)

One Sunday when this passage was the Gospel for the day, a woman leaving the early service met a friend who was arriving for the later service. She asked, "Are you still having the family and your husband's friends for his surprise birthday dinner?"

"Of course," her friend replied.

"Well," the first woman said, "you're going to have trouble with the Gospel for today."

Is that what this means? That dinner for family and friends are anathema to our Lord? I don't think so. Jesus often ate with friends. Rather, it seems clear, we are chiefly to keep in mind the fourteenth verse: "Blessed are you because they cannot repay you."

Much of our social intercourse — too much, most of the time — is based on reciprocal arrangements. We must invite the Smiths and the Joneses because we owe them. They had us for dinner since we last invited them. We must invite the Greens and the Thompsons because they can be helpful in landing that contract we're after. "You scratch my back and I'll scratch yours" is often — too often, most of the time — the basis for doing what we do.

Jesus saw this happening then, and we see it happening now. In the midst of our reciprocal arrangements he asks the uncomfortable question: What are we doing for those who cannot repay us? Some of us, like the Pharisees, would be hard put to answer. After all, who wants to eat with *that* kind of people? So, we do much of our "charity," our "benevolence" on an impersonal basis. Our Christian duty is done and we can forget it.

*He dropped a dollar in the plate
And meekly raised his eyes,
Glad that the weekly rent was paid
For his mansion in the skies.*

Of course, our benevolence is necessary and good; but what are we giving of *ourselves* to those who cannot repay us?

One of the prayers in the book of worship in the church to which I belong puts it this way: "O, Lord, help us to remember those who are so easy to forget — the homeless, the destitute, the sick, the aged and all those who have no one to care for them." Those who are so easy to forget were high on Jesus' list. They need to have a place on ours.

Jesus is not talking about social life, but about *Christian* social life, and that's different. Is he saying we can't have cousin Effie for lunch or have a family gathering at Thanksgiving? No, but if that's *all* we do — if we divorce ourselves as persons from other people's needs as persons — we are missing Jesus' mandate. Christian love is not adequately expressed with dollar bills and keeping our distance.

This is the pointed thrust of the passage: what are we doing *personally* for those who cannot repay us? In our sharing, what are we sharing *of ourselves?* These are often disturbing questions to ask ourselves, but if we are Jesus' disciples they are questions we must ask and answer — to ourselves and to him.

All in all, it was not a comfortable dinner that day, but we can hope some attitudes toward humility and sharing were changed. Given some of our attitudes on status and benevolence, it may not be comfortable for us to read about it today either. Still, we can hope it may change some of our attitudes as well.

O, Lord, help us to remember those who it is so easy to forget — those who need not only our charity, but our love and concern, our faith and our Lord. Amen

Luke 14:25-33

Proper 18 (C)
Pentecost 16 (L)
Ordinary Time 23 (RC)

I Voted for God

The Gospel for today begins with these words of Jesus:

Now great multitudes accompanied him; and he turned and said to them, "If any one comes to me and does not hate his own father and mother and wife and children and brothers and sisters, yes, and even his own life, he cannot be my disciple."

Is that what it means to be a Christian? That we should hate the members of our own family? We must make allowances here not only for the circumstances, but also for the fact that Eastern language is sharp and vivid and dramatic. In Matthew's Gospel it is stated this way:

Jesus said, "He that loves father and mother more than me is not worthy of me; and he that loves son or daughter more than me is not worthy of me."

Still and all, it's a pretty stringent requirement. Honestly now, if you were to make a list at this moment on the blank margin or your church bulletin of those you loved the most, in preferential order, on how many lists would Jesus' name be first? If this is the requirement, do I qualify as a disciple, as over against a "follower"?

Why would Jesus use such harsh language in his warning to the crowd? Why was the crowd there at all? One reason, of course, was curiosity. The news about this Galilean — the things he did and the words he spoke — had spread along the

Palestinian grapevine. What would he say, and what would he do next? So they gaped at him and trailed after him, something like the way we moderns do to a movie star or a sports luminary or a politician. Jesus used these words like a thresher's flail to separate the wheat from the chaff.

The second reason for the crowd is this: When Jesus spoke these words he was on his way to Jerusalem and then to the Cross. Patriots in the crowd thought he was their champion on the way to a throne, so they "accompanied" him. They were "with him" physically and emotionally. As his "followers" they would expect to receive his favors. They were following him not only for the excitement, but for the possible perquisites. In this circumstance they needed a stern admonition, and he gave it: they should rather be counting the cost. It is essential but disconcerting to ask ourselves whether we might need the same admonition. With Jesus' words in mind, can we qualify for discipleship? Our Lord's concern was that those who were following him for the possible perquisites should rather be counting the cost. Is such an admonition relevant to his followers today?

It is this second reason that poses the greatest danger to us. Jesus is no longer much of a curiosity now, but he is still one from whom great blessings seem possible, and often are received. We need to hear his warnings that these blessings are not cheap, but rather carry the cost of commitment. To separate the followers from the disciples he uses his examples of the builder and the warrior — stressing the need to count the cost of the venture of discipleship.

Today, as then, he has many "followers" — millions of members of the Christian churches — but few disciples. Look at any church record of attendance or stewardship of time, talent and substance. What is the percentage of those who put Jesus first? There are still plenty of people who seek the blessings but are either not counting the cost or are not willing to pay it. Such people seek the cheap "no commitment" blessings he does not offer. Such seeking ends in disappointment and disillusionment. That's why lots of his "followers" get discouraged with him in our day, just as they did in his day.

One of the facts of political life is patronage. When a party member works and contributes and votes for a candidate, he expects to get something out of it — a contract for his company, a job for his son, help in getting a bill passed. We accept it as a matter of course in political life. However, unfortunately this attitude carries over into other areas of life. For example, our community honored one of its famous citizens with a huge banquet for six hundred people. This person has many friends and even more "followers." It would be extremely difficult to compose a guest list. With that many involved there were bound to be some mix-ups.

On the day after the dinner I remarked to a friend in casual conversation, "I received two invitations, and I don't know why. I have not contributed to the cause."

He replied, "I have contributed several times, and I received no invitation." Then he added this significant statement: "Of course, they'll never get another dime from me. You see? I voted for them. Where is my patronage?"

It is most unfortunate when this attitude carries over into our relationship with God. Some of us look on our church membership and occasional contributions as a vote for Jesus. Sometimes we look on our church attendance as a favor to God or the minister, and on our prayers as a bargaining session with God. It becomes a give-and-take experience. I am voting for Jesus. Where is my patronage?

We talk a lot about the Christian life being no guarantee of specific dispensation, but many of us can't quite seem to accept the idea. The Christian life does not protect us from our own incompetence, our own sin and our own foolishness. It does not protect us from the malice and evil in other people, nor from ill health and death. There is much seeming injustice in the world. Sometimes we are its victims, and we want to know why. I vote for Jesus. Where is my patronage? Many of us can't seem to shake the idea.

A man was in a serious accident. He said to his pastor, "When the doctors told me I would not be able to walk properly or drive my car for a year I nearly lost my faith." Translation: "I've always been good. Why does this happen to me?"

Even some of those who agree with it mentally do not seem to be able to accept it for themselves. For example, a devout and extremely active church woman in our city heard about a small child who was dying. She organized a group of two hundred church members to pray for the child. "We are going to save that child." The child died. She is now no longer a devout woman. She said, "If God won't hear the prayers of two hundred of his people, if he will not save the life of a little child, he does not exist."

I met a man in the steam bath recently. When he learned that I was a minister he said, "My luck has been terrible lately. I tried everything to change it. I even joined the church, but it didn't help any." You see? I voted for Jesus. Where is my patronage? It's the old cry from Calvary, "If you are the Christ, save yourself and us."

Discouragement, disillusionment, but not discipleship. Tradition and church history tell us that all of Christ's disciples save one died a violent death for their faith. Only John escaped martyrdom.* Not discouragement, not disillusionment, but discipleship.

The mark of a great leader is that he sets the terms of his discipleship. In his *Idylls of the King,* Tennyson tells us that King Arthur bound his knights "by so straight vows that they were dazed as if half blinded by the coming of a light." Garibaldi offered his men only hunger and death to free Italy. Winston Churchill promised the English people only "blood, sweat and tears" to resist the Nazi invader.

*Andrew died on a cross
Bartholomew was flayed alive
James (son of Zebedee) was beheaded
Simon was crucified
James (son of Alphaeus) was beaten to death
Thomas was run through with a lance
Matthias was stoned and beheaded
Matthew was slain by the sword
Peter was crucified head downward
Thaddeus was shot to death with arrows
Philip was hanged

Jesus makes no bones about the cost of discipleship to him. He makes no false and easy promises. In our witnessing and in our evangelism we should not do it either. A man in Miami, named Hugh NcNatt, sued the Allapattah Baptist church and its minister to get his offerings back. He said the minister promised blessings, benefits and rewards would come if he tithed. They didn't come so he wanted his money back. He obviously voted for Jesus and wanted his patronage.

The message of today's Gospel seems clear. Christian discipleship is not a matter of social conformity, personal convenience, economic advantage or escape from the harsh realities of life. It is to love the Lord Jesus above all else. It is to find that his presence is our blessing, our strength against temptation, our joy in serving others and our victory over whatever life might bring.

When I read today's Gospel I think I hear, in my own heart as well as some of yours, the plaint of those early disciples, "Who then, can be saved?" (Matthew 19:25) I know no other answer than the one he gave to them: "With men this is impossible. With God all things are possible." It's the only hope we have.

Help us to love and serve you for what you are, our Lord and Savior, not for what we might get from you. Lead us on the path of commitment and discipleship, that we might know the joy of your presence as we love and serve other people in your name. Amen

Luke 15:1-10

Proper 19 (C)
Pentecost 17 (L)
Ordinary Time 24 (RC)

Dodging the Thrust

Jesus was the companion of sinners. Companion? Yes. We get our word "companion" from "com" (*with*) and "panis" (*food*). A companion is someone you eat with. Jesus was the companion of sinners.

Who were these "sinners"? We'd have a difficult time pinning the label, having, as we do, Paul's reminder to the Romans, "For all have sinned and come short of the glory of God." (Romans 3:23) The Pharisees had no such problem. For them it was simple: a sinner was any person who did not observe the details of the orthodox law. Jesus wanted sinners to know God. The Pharisees did not. They didn't seek them — they shunned them. They even had a name for them. They called them "the people of the land."

It would be easy today to dodge the thrust of this Gospel. The first dodge might be this: we could talk about sheep and shepherds; about coins and the floor of Palestinian homes. There would be several interesting things to say.

For example: the shepherd was responsible for the sheep. If a sheep was lost, the shepherd must at least bring home the fleece to show how it had died. The shepherds were experts at tracking and could follow the footprints of a straying sheep a long way. It was often part of the day's work for a shepherd to risk his life for the sheep. A straying sheep could lose its landmarks and bleat helplessly at the edge of a precipice.

Another example: it would be easy to lose a coin in most

Palestinian homes of that day. Most of the houses were dark. The floors were beaten earth covered with dried reeds and rushes. It was easy to lose a coin. Perhaps it was necessary for the woman to find it out of economic necessity; or perhaps because it was one of ten silver coins linked together by a chain that formed the necklace of the headdress of a married woman, something like our wedding ring today. Who knows?

Jesus is not talking primarily about sheep and coins. He's talking about persons who need the Lord. We can't dodge it.

A second dodge might be to take comfort in the percentages of the story. For the shepherd, one sheep out of a flock of one hundred was a one percent loss. That's not too bad, but it's no use telling that to the shepherd. He leaves the ninety and nine — a risky act in itself — and seeks the one until he finds it, as though it were the only sheep that mattered. Each one had a place in his care. There is joy in his heart when he finds it.

For the woman, it was one coin out of ten, a ten-percent loss. Yet how can a wife joyfully wear the headdress with one coin missing? She seeks the coin as though it were the only one that mattered. Each coin had a place in the bridal strand. There is joy in her heart when she finds it.

Or, we might take comfort in the percentages of the statistics of the church. From twelve disciples it has grown to millions of members. Or consider the percentage of people in the church in relation to other things. For example, there are more people in church on any given Sunday than at all the professional Sunday football games for a whole year. Or consider the high percentage of people on the rolls of the churches who are faithful in communion and contribution compared to the lower percentage of those who drift away.

Can we honestly talk about percentages to the Jesus who told about the shepherd and the housewife and about the joy in heaven over one sinner that repents? Jesus is not talking about percentages, but about persons who do not know the Lord. We can't dodge it that way.

A third dodge might be to talk about people, to point the finger of scorn, like the Pharisees did. For example, we could talk about the three young men who live in a nearby apartment. My goodness! The way they talk, the things they do! Such carrying on!

A woman who lived in a small town often went shopping in the big city some distance away. She assured her children that she couldn't get lost. She had certain landmarks. She always knew the way home, and how close to home she was getting. Then they put in the new highway. She said, "Now I never know quite where I am, or how close I am to home. I've lost my landmarks."

Perhaps those three young men, like that woman and like some sheep, have lost their landmarks, too — the home of their childhood, the gospel hymns in the little church, the mother who heard their childhood bedtime prayers. Oh, yes, we could talk about people, and point the finger of scorn, like the Pharisees did.

For example, there is that family that moved in across the street. They argue a lot. Their children are often left alone. If they go to church, I've never noticed it. Who are they? Did they leave their landmarks back home with their roots and their friends? In the strange geography of a new town, in the unaccustomed isolation of having no one who seems to care, have they lost their landmarks too?

We could talk about people, and point the finger of scorn; but Jesus was not talking about "people," but rather about *persons*, and that's different. He was not talking about coins, but *a* coin; not about sheep, but about *a* sheep — and in each case it was found by a person who cared. We can't dodge it that way.

The thrust of this Gospel is toward us. It is a pointed question: Do we care about persons who do not know the Lord? There's not much use in our telling them they are lost. They may not know it, like the coin, or may not realize it, like the sheep. If we told those three young men they were lost they might laugh at us, or give us a smart remark. If we told that family across the street they were lost, they might tell us to mind our own business or snap that they are just as good as we are. It's not much use telling them they are lost.

Do we care enough to exhibit the Christian life as best we can, with persistent acts of caring and kindness? Do we care enough to tell them what Jesus means to us, and could mean to them? Do we care enough to let them laugh, and give us a smart answer if they will; to let them tell us to mind our own business and remind us of our own shortcomings if they will? At least they will know someone cares — the way Jesus did.

Through our caring, the Holy Spirit may do his work. The knowledge and the memory that someone cared may be like a grain of sand in an oyster, which will grow into a pearl. The results are in God's hands, not ours, if we have done what we could. If we have *not* cared, if we have *not* done what we could, then, as Ezekiel puts it, "their blood be on us." (Ezekiel 33:7-9)

While visiting in the hospital I met a little nine-year-old girl who was a patient. I thought I recognized her name, so I asked her if she was the little girl by that name who went to our Sunday church school. She replied, "No, Sir. I don't go anywhere to Sunday church school."

I told her who I was and said, "While I'm here perhaps we could have a prayer."

She replied, "That would be fine, but I don't know any prayers." Nine years old!

I said, "What I meant was that I would offer a prayer for you."

She replied, "That would be fine. No one has ever prayed for me before." Nine years old!

Of course, I followed up on that little girl. In the house on one side of her home lived a family nominally members of a major Christian denomination. In the house on the other side lived a family nominally a member of another denomination, and two of our own families lived in the same block with that little girl. That little girl also lives in your city and perhaps in your block — no matter where you live — and the Jesus who told about the sheep and the coin asks us, "Do you care?"

How can we be complacent about our Christian faith as long as we know persons who have wandered away from the Lord like coins? The church has all kinds of evangelism programs, committees, workshops, literature; but all of it is not much good without the essential ingredient — someone who cares that a person does not know the Lord.

The sheep was not scolded, the coin was not cursed — they were sought after by someone who cared. Forget the statistics. Most of us know someone who does not know the Lord. Do we care?

This Gospel is not simply aimed at the Pharisees. It is aimed at us; and the thrust of its message is : *Do you care?* It's no use trying to dodge it. It doesn't matter who they are, where they are or how they got lost. We have one message, to be expressed in quiet words and in compassionate kindness: "Jesus cares about you."

Who on God's green earth is going to tell them if we Christians don't?

Dear Lord, bring into our minds today the name of someone who does not know you as Jesus revealed you. Nudge us to do something about it. Keep us restless and disturbed until we do. Remind us that all we need to do is speak the kindly word about Jesus and do the kindly act in his name. The results are in your hands. Amen

Luke 16:1-13 *Proper 20 (C)*
Pentecost 18 (L)
Ordinary Time 25 (RC)

Jesus and the Rascal

Why in the world would Jesus tell this story? On casual reading it seems as though he is making a hero out of a villain. What does it mean? To help us answer that we put the spotlight on three verses; but first, a bit of background.

In Palestine there were absentee landlords who employed overseers to manage the property in their absence. The tenants paid their rents "in kind" — that is, with a portion of their produce; in this case, a hundred measures of oil, a hundred measures of wheat. Any thought that Jesus lived in an ivory tower, unaware of the hard and often sordid facts of life, is banished by this parable.

This overseer was a rascal. There can be no doubt about that. He wasted his master's goods and he falsified the entries in his master's books. Furthermore, he was dealing with a lot of other rascals, and he knew it.

First, turn the spotlight on verse two. The master called the steward and said, "Turn in the account of your stewardship, for you can no longer be steward." As the steward discovered, tomorrow really *does* come. For better or for worse, tomorrow is loaded with the inescapable consequences of today. Robert Louis Stevenson wrote, "Everybody soon or late sits down to a banquet of consequences." Tomorrow is God's judgment on today.

A man bought a parrot. He taught that bird to say one

word. That word was, "Today." When he got up in the morning and when he came home at night it was beaten into his eardrums: "Today." There was no procrastination around that bird. "Today, today, today," he screamed.

About six months later the man bought another parrot. He taught that bird to say one word. That word was "Tomorrow." He said, "I have been living as if there were no future. Today is all there is, and I've found it isn't so." The two birds together helped him keep his mind on the realities of life: today and tomorrow. Would that the steward could have heard both voices. Tomorrow is God's judgment on today.

Today is important. It is the only time we can call our own. God's Word is full of the significance of today. The psalmist wrote, "This is the day the Lord has made. Let us rejoice and be glad in it." (Psalm 118:24) Paul wrote to the Corinthians, "Behold, now is the acceptable time. Now is the day of salvation." (2 Corinthians 6:2) We are to live *today* — but not only *for* today. Tomorrow does come. We, too, are only stewards — of life itself and all that it contains. We need both words, for we also, like this ancient overseer, must give an account of our stewardship.

Second, turn the spotlight on verse eight. The first part reads, "The master commended the dishonest steward for his prudence." Here is where a casual reading could lead us astray. You remember what the steward did: he cheated the master by doctoring the books. He changed the bills from one-hundred measures of oil to fifty, and from one-hundred measures of wheat to eighty so that they would be beholden to him when he was no longer steward. We must remember that the master commended the steward *not* for his criminal rascality, but for his prudence. He handled his material calamity with resourcefulness (even though it was dishonest). He did the best he could with the circumstances that beset him, handling them with diligence and foresight. Jesus is telling his disciples that they are to serve God like that. The "children of light" are to have the same wisdom and foresight in serving God as the "children of this world" have in serving themselves.

The "children of this world" are not necessarily rascals. They are simply those whose main concern is material things. They serve their own interest above all else. They have little or no concern with spiritual things, or with other people's welfare. With time and patience, with diligence and foresight they serve material things in their own interest!

As the "children of light" whose chief concern is supposedly with spiritual things and with other people's needs — kindness, love, prayer and their relationship with God — as the "children of light," how does our wisdom and foresight compare with theirs? Do we study our Bibles with the same diligence and persistence as the computer operator and the insurance man study their manuals? Do we devote time and patience to our prayers and our witnessing like the investor to his accounts or the sportsman to his skills?

Jesus said, "In the world you shall have tribulation." (John 16:33) When *our* calamities come — illness, sorrow, injustice, disappointment or misfortune — we are to handle them with the same wisdom and foresight with which the crooked steward handled his calamity. We are not to let them rob us of our trust in God's power and love.

For example, when Leland Stanford lost his son, he did not handle the calamity with bitterness and resignation. Out of his heartache he built a school for other boys. It has become one of America's great universities. He handled his calamity with wisdom and foresight. He did not let his sorrow rob him of his trust in God's power and love.

Third, the spotlight shines the brightest on verse thirteen. "No servant can serve two masters; for either he will hate the one and love the other, or he will be devoted to the one and despise the other. You cannot serve God and mammon."

Jesus is using strong language here to press the importance of his point. He is not making a judgment; he is stating a fact. He does not say, "You *ought* not"; he says, "You *cannot*." Perhaps a closer reading of his words would be, "no man can be a slave to two owners."

The word "mammon" itself simply means "material things." Like other words, its meaning changed somewhat as time went by. It later referred to material things *entrusted* to someone to keep safe for him, like this steward, or like a banker. Gradually it came to mean *things in which a person puts his trust,* and was regarded as an evil god. So Jesus is saying, "You cannot put your complete trust in God and material things." It had of necessity to be one or the other. Complete trust in either naturally excludes the other.

Jesus does not teach that it is necessarily wrong to *have* material things, but it is wrong (and futile, one might add) to put one's *trust* in material things. All of us, of necessity, deal with the material things of life. The question is not how much or how little of this world's goods we have, but what our *attitude* is *toward* them, what we *believe about* them and what we *do with* them. They are to be our servants, not our masters. When we arrange our life around them, treasure them above integrity, friendship, honesty and generosity, they have become our master. No person can be a slave to two masters.

When we use money, and the other material things of life which money can buy, in order to accomplish good purposes, we are on solid Christian ground. We thus provide for our needs, provide for the family and help other people. But when, as so often happens, we desire things just to have more things (not to live *on,* but to live *for*), then mammon has become our master. It has then become, as the ancients called it, a little god, and has taken the place that only God should have. So Jesus says, "You cannot be a servant of these two masters." We choose our ultimate allegiance. We reveal that choice by what we do with what has been entrusted to our care by God or by other people.

A man in California plunged into his burning house and threw out his securities, but did not escape himself. He sacrificed his security for his securities, and he lost them both.

God is the only capitalist, the ultimate owner. In everything we are overseers of *his* wealth. The wealth this rascal wrongfully used was not his own, but his master's. The things we use, rightly or wrongfully — time, talent and possessions — are not our own, but God's. In everything we are stewards, not owners.

A little girl, romping through fields of wildflowers, was reminded how wonderful God is to provide us with such beautiful fields. She asked, "Do you think God would mind if I picked some of his flowers?" She had the right idea.

Now the spotlight shifts once more. It shines on you and on me. Having material things — little or much — is not a sin, but a danger. The danger is this: the more things we have, the more inclined we are to put our trust in them, to give them the place that only God should have, and thus to be a slave to mammon. The possession of things — little or much — is a matter for prayer, in order that they may be our servants, and never be allowed to become our masters; prayer that they may be used as the owner God would have them used.

No matter how we sugar-coat it or try to evade it, this is the cold, hard fact as Jesus stated it. No person can serve two masters. We cannot put our trust in God and mammon. It is not that we *ought* not, but rather that we *cannot*. It sounds simple, but true happiness, peace of mind and eternity depend on which one it is.

"Today" and "tomorrow" — we need both words in our ears every day. Parrots we may not have, but somehow, deep inside us the words they spoke need to reverberate. Like this overseer of old, we modern overseers must give an account of our allegiance when God says, in the words of this Gospel, "Turn in the account of your stewardship."

Our Father, we are constantly surrounded by the acquisition of, and the need for, material things. Help us to acquire them honestly and use them wisely, as in your sight. Save us from being rascally stewards of your bounty. In Jesus' name. Amen

Luke 16:19-31 *Proper 21 (C)*
Pentecost 19 (L)
Ordinary Time 26 (RC)

The Man Who Didn't Care

A woman once said to her pastor, "I enjoy your Bible classes very much. You get so much out of the text that isn't there." What she meant, of course, was that he saw and explained things that were not evident to her.

Let's take her literally for a moment. As we study the Gospel for today, let's get out of it some of the things that are *not* there in order to see clearly the things that *are* there. It's easy to read some unwarranted meanings into this parable — like putting on a suit of armor to keep the real point of the story from jabbing us. Let's take off that armor of unwarranted meanings and expose ourselves to its possibly painful prodding of our personal Christian living.

1. This is not a condemnation of wealth. "Dives" is the Latin word for "rich," and this man certainly was. He was "clothed in purple" — the outer garment dyed with costly purple murex — and "fine linen" — the under garment woven from Egyptian flax. Jesus knew the circumstances of the rich as well as the poor. This was no occasional banquet. The rich man feasted sumptuously every day. Here is a solid citizen, a man of wealth and social standing. That was not his sin. There is here no condemnation of his wealth. After all, Abraham was wealthy, too.

2. This is not a praise of poverty. A beggar "lay" at the

portico of his palatial home, evidently carried there by someone else. His name was Lazarus (in Hebrew, "Eleazar"), meaning "he whom God helps." Such was his poverty that his rags could not cover his ulcerated body. When dogs came and bothered him, he had no strength to drive them away. He begged for the discarded pieces of bread the diners had used as napkins to wipe their hands and mouths.

Lazarus died. There is no mention of his burial; perhaps it was in some potter's field. When Dives died, Jesus says he was "buried." Perhaps it was a first class funeral, with wailing hired mourners, befitting his station in life. Not all beggars are godly people, but we can assume Lazarus' godliness since he was carried to Abraham's bosom. Whether he deserved compassion or not, Jesus does not say. It doesn't make any difference. The point is not his deserving, but his need.

3. This is *not* a factual description of heaven and hell. Jesus believed in heaven and hell but made no attempt to describe them. "Abraham's bosom" was the ancient Jewish term for heaven (something like our "Pearly Gates" expression), and Hades was the expression for separation from God. These are symbols, and we must not make them "proofs" of a fire and brimstone hell.

There are here, however, indications of the nature of eternal life: there is self-consciousness (death is not oblivion, even though some people might wish it were); there is memory (life is not "water over the dam"); there is recognition (knowing one another is possible, even across the gulf that Jesus describes).

4. This is *not* evidence of Dives' loving concern for his five brothers. It is rather a clever camouflage to excuse himself. You see? His predicament is God's fault. Who could expect anyone to be convinced on only the say-so of Moses and the prophets? *He* hadn't. But if one came from the dead, *that* would save his brothers. That would have saved *him*, is the

implication. It's God's fault for not pushing him harder. If he'd only known! And God should have *made* him know.

We may be inclined to agree with his estimate that his brothers would be reformed if one came to them from the dead; but they wouldn't, of course. They — or we — might gape in wonder, and quake with fear at such an event, but these emotions would soon pass. As with other fears and wonders, time would soften the impact and the old self would soon assert itself again. They had God's revelation of himself for their day — Moses and the prophets — which they chose to ignore. We have even more — God's revelation of himself for our day — his Word, which we can read every day; witnesses, past and present, of the power of his saving love; Jesus himself dying on the Cross. At Calvary God shot his last bolt in man's redemption. These are our "Moses and the prophets," for us either to accept or ignore.

Nobody deliberately *intends* to go to hell. How and why, then, do people go? Almost nobody *believes* he is going to hell. Those who are not confident in the victory of their faith in Jesus as their personal Savior fall back on the hope and belief that there is no such hellish life after death at all. Maybe Dives felt that way. What a rude awakening!

Now that we have cleared away some of the brush, let's look at some of the teachings that *are* in this story Jesus told.

1. Jesus makes it clear that there *is* a life beyond this world of five senses; that God rules both worlds; and that life in one world affects the other. Jesus' teaching on heaven and the hungry recorded in Saint Matthew (25:31-46) is an underlining of this same idea. What we do in this life of five senses affects the life beyond them; not because we are making "brownie points" with God, but because each of us is becoming a certain kind of individual who belongs in a certain kind of environment.

For example, here is a person who attends church faithfully, serves his neighbors unselfishly, donates blood, tithes, reads good books — including *the* Good Book — and enjoys the fellowship of those who, like himself, love the Lord. This person is moved by his employer to a distant community. In his new community he will probably seek the same environment — because he *is* that kind of person. He has been fitting himself for that kind of environment. That's where he is at home. That's where he belongs. It is something like that between this life of five senses and the life beyond. Each of us is creating the kind of person who is at home being with God and the environment of God, or is at home separated from God and the things that belong to God's environment.

2. Jesus says that between these two environments a great separation is fixed — an unbridgeable chasm, he puts it in our worldly language. Who digs this chasm? Dives himself had driven a wedge of selfishness between himself and his needy fellows, therefore between himself and God. First there is an act, then a habit, then a character trait — until there is a gap so wide that Jesus says even heaven itself could not bridge it.

The clearest evidence of what we believe about God is the way we treat other people. Godly acts of goodness, generosity and compassion — or their opposites — are not simply acts in themselves. They are the outward evidence that the person who performs them is a certain kind of person. If we meanly treat our needy fellows — if we are callous and careless of their condition or their needs — we separate ourselves from them. In doing so, we separate ourselves from God.

Dives walked past Lazarus just about every day, but he did not really "see" him at all. Lazarus' needs were obvious, but Dives just didn't care. It was not what Dives *did* that got him into hell; it was what he did *not* do.

3. It comes down to this: *we* are the brothers of Dives, those whose eternal destiny is yet to be determined. What kind of persons are we becoming?

Dives was evidently not actively evil, deliberately devilish or consciously cruel. He was just carelessly heartless. He had lost his compassion. He had buried his brotherhood. Rags and ulcers left him unmoved and uncaring. They were merely a part of the other man's tough luck, and no concern of his.

There are people who don't care what happens as long as it doesn't happen to them. Either we are men and women of compassion, of caring and concern, or we are men and women of hell. That's pretty blunt, but on the basis of this story, how else would you put it?

We can be concerned about poverty, ghetto conditions, disease, injustice, fear and loneliness (even though these things do not happen to us), or we can shrug our shoulders and say, "What is that to me?" The difference between those two attitudes is not a minor matter. Here Jesus makes it the difference between heaven and hell.

The sharp point of Jesus' story is this: we need not be actively evil or deliberately devilish to miss the gate of heaven. We need only to be inactively indifferent and thoughtlessly selfish; to go our own contented way; to step over the beggars on the doorstep of our life, unconcerned about their condition and untroubled about their need.

There is a sign series on the West Virginia Turnpike that says, "Driving while drowsy can put you to sleep — permanently." Drowsy, uncaring living can put us to sleep — permanently. That kind of person, Jesus says, is separating himself from God until it becomes permanent, by digging a chasm between himself and heaven that even the love of God cannot bridge.

Open our eyes, Lord, to the needs and sufferings of those around us. Even though we may not have caused the hurts we see, grant us compassionate hearts to respond to them, that we might be the kind of people who belong eternally with you. Amen

Luke 17:5-10 (C, RC) Proper 22 (C)
Luke 17:1-10 (L) Pentecost 20 (L)
  Ordinary Time 27 (RC)

No Snap Courses

More than a century ago Sydney Smith wrote in his *Lady Holland's Memoir* these disturbing words: "Whoever wishes to imply the absence of everything agreeable and inviting, he calls it a sermon." How shall we escape that indictment today?

When we read verses seven through ten in today's Gospel, it is somewhat shocking to read that Jesus said this in describing our relationship with God. We must remember, however, that like most parables, this is only a partial view of God. There is no mention here, for example, of God's love and forgiveness.

These words of Jesus show a knowledgeable and realistic picture of rural Palestinian life in his day. Here he is neither commending nor condemning the master's treatment of his servants. He is merely describing what was to them a well-known situation. Jesus always had a reason for his teaching, and these forceful words are no exception. Let's look at his obvious purpose in telling this parable to the disciples of both his day and of ours.

I

It is a warning that following Jesus simply in the expectation of cheap blessings and comfort is to miss much of the responsibility and obligation of discipleship. It is evident in many places in the Gospels that Jesus was well aware that some of those who followed him were doing so out of ignorance of what was expected of them. They were unaware of the nature and the cost of discipleship. There was a discussion even among the twelve as to who should be greatest among them. (Luke 9:46) James and John were interested that they should sit one at his right hand and one at his left when he came into his glory. (Mark 10:35-45)

When Jesus said, "The foxes have holes and birds of the air have nests; but the Son of Man has nowhere to lay his head" (Luke 9:58), one would-be follower backed off, saying, "Suffer me first to bury my father." He meant that he couldn't keep on with Jesus as long as his father was alive. One excuse is as good as another. When the one we have called the "rich young ruler" heard the cost of following Jesus, he "turned away sorrowing." (Matthew 19:22)

It is inevitable that this misunderstanding of the cost of discipleship should be present in our day as well. A missionary was telling his audience about the wondrous love and forgiveness of God. He used the story of the prodigal son. One young tribesman came up to him afterward and said, "Master, *I* am the prodigal son." The missionary was pleased at this response — glad that the seed of the Word had taken root. However, the young man waited expectantly, and after a few moments asked, "Master, where is my fatted calf?" He needed to hear, as many of us do, the cost — the duty, the obligation of being a disciple of Jesus. The blessings follow that.

In our discussions of the Christian life we tend to emphasize its joy, its peace of mind, its awareness of forgiveness. This is a stern warning that following Jesus is not simply being a kindly personality and joining a happiness cult. There *is* a joy, a sense of forgiveness, a peace of mind that comes from believing in Jesus as our personal Savior. There *is* a certain winsomeness as we see the Christian life in action — its patience, its kindness, its love, its forgiveness and its generosity.

However, there is another side to it too. There is that which is expected of those who would be his disciples. This is one of the places where Jesus tells us what it is. He uses the hard, unyielding word "duty." The dictionary says that a *duty* is "something we ought to do." It is not a choice, but an obligation. In these verses Jesus tells us that it is a rigorous duty indeed. There is no room for pride in what we do for God. As Christians, our main concern is obedience, and the word "obedience," like the word "duty," does not fall pleasantly on our ears. We live in a democracy where those two words are seldom used. All the more, then, do we need to hear these words from Jesus. We need to think less about our blessings *from* God and more about our *duty* as Christians *toward* God.

II

These verses remind us that the nature of God is complex, even as we who are made in his image are complex. Like a beautiful diamond, the nature of God has many facets. Jesus here reveals an aspect of God's nature which we may not like, but which we need to see. Jesus has shown that God, as revealed in him, is a loving father, an understanding, forgiving Lord, a suffering servant whose followers shall not walk in darkness, but who have the light of life. (John 8:12)

Here he declares that God is not only loving, he is expectant. He is not only patient, he is demanding. One who sets his hand to the plow and hesitantly looks back is not worthy of the Kingdom of God. (Luke 9:62) God is easy to please, but hard to satisfy. Serving our Lord is a relentless and unending task. In our choosing of, and our discussion about, Christian discipleship, we must not neglect to include this facet of the nature of God.

III

This parable keeps us from being proud of our virtues or smug in our goodness. We are only doing what is expected of us. These verses keep us from self-pity in our sorrows, our setbacks and our hardships. The words, "I've always been a good person. Why does this happen to me?" should never be on our lips.

We are only doing what is expected of us. The rest is in God's hands. Look back over your school days, when you were a learner. From whom did you learn the most? Whose teachings lingered the longest? Whose demands best prepared you for life? The easy teachers or the hard taskmasters?

A high school teacher who confides in me is reported to be what the students call a "tough teacher." There are no easy grades. The assignments are completed — or else! She is constant in encouragement, plentiful in patience, generous in help, *but demanding in performance.* She tells me that her students often groan and sigh — but they work and they learn. When those students go on to college, to whom do they telephone (long distance yet, and at their own expense!) to exult that they are far ahead of their fellow students in those particular courses? Whom do they come back to visit, to say "thank you" for making them become what they are in their college courses? To the "tough teacher," of course. It was not the easy, but the demanding, teacher who made something out of them, students fit for a college degree.

Does today's Gospel sound as though God is a hard taskmaster? The word "disciple" comes from the Latin word meaning "learner." To be a disciple means to be not only a "follower" but a "learner." We are learners of the lessons of life and eternity, lessons that prepare us for God's heart and home.

So we are back to Sydney Smith's indictment, that with which we began: "Whoever wishes to imply the absence of everything agreeable and inviting, he calls it a sermon." Can we be charged with that today? Yet it is not I, but our Lord himself, who laid the basis for our discussion. Evidently Jesus believed his followers ought to hear it. We would much rather read about and hear about God's love and forgiveness and blessings than we would about his demands. As those who name the name of Jesus and set our footsteps on the road to heaven, we need to remember that God does his labor of love and life, not through snap courses, but through demanding assignments. From the word "disciple" we get our word "discipline." The Gospel for today reveals God's discipline.

The Christian hope is that God, through Jesus, can make something out of us that's fit to be with him. This is the way he does it.

Who answers Christ's insistent call
Must give himself, his life, his all,
Without the backward look;
Who sets his hand unto the plow
And glances back with anxious brow
His calling hath mistook.
Christ claims him wholly for His own;
He must be Christ's and Christ's alone.

*John Oxenham (*quoted in the
Expositor's Minister's Annual 1930)

"So you also, when you have done all that is commanded of you, say "We are unworthy servants; we have only done what was our duty."

Teach us who are learners, O Lord, the lessons of life that prepare us for eternity. We who are the disciples of Jesus claim his patience and forgiveness toward us and bask in his love for us. Help us to accept the whole Jesus. Forbid it that we should shrink from his claims on us. By your Holy Spirit strengthen us in the dutiful service he demands. We ask it in his name. Amen

About the Author

Carveth P. Mitchell was born in Cornwall, England. He received his early education in England and in Detroit, Michigan. He was graduated from Wittenberg University, Springfield, Ohio, with a B.A. Degree and from Hamma School of Theology with the B.D. Degree. He received the Doctor of Divinity from Wittenberg University.

Dr. Mitchell is a popular banquet speaker having done this for national conventions of various industrial and professional groups. He has had speaking tours in many countries of the world in behalf of the United States Air Force — in Europe, the Far East and the South Pacific. He has conducted preaching missions on many air bases in America and in various colleges, communities and churches throughout the country.

He has served as a member of the Board of Social Ministry of the Lutheran Church in America, as Chairman of its Evangelism division, and as Chairman of the Board of Directors of the Lutheran Church in America Foundation.

As a member of the Synod of Ohio he served on its Executive Board and as a member of the Board of Directors of Wittenberg University and Hamma School of Theology. He has served the North Carolina Synod as a member of its Executive Board, the Board of Directors of Lutheran Theological Seminary and the Synodical Stewardship committee. He currently serves as an Evangel for the Synod. He has been a regular panelist on the television programs "Perspective" and "Pastors Face Your Questions."

For 19 years he was Pastor of First Lutheran Church, Mansfield, Ohio. In 1963 he became Pastor of Saint Mark's Lutheran Church, Charlotte, North Carolina, where he served until his retirement. He currently teaches Public Speaking and Parliamentary Law at Queen's College in the Adult Education department. He is the author of numerous articles and one book, *No Silent Saints*.

He is married to Kathryn (nee Rogers). Their son, Sandford Carveth Mitchell, is the senior pastor of Trinity Lutheran Church, Ashland, Ohio. Their daughter, Kathryn Ann Taylor, is head of the English Department at Providence Day High School in Charlotte, North Carolina.

www.ingramcontent.com/pod-product-compliance
Lightning Source LLC
Chambersburg PA
CBHW060852050426
42453CB00008B/949